AF605480

Original Korean text by Mi-ae Lee
Illustrations by Yeon-joo Kim

This English edition published by big & SMALL in 2016
by arrangement with Aram Publishing
English text edited by Joy Cowley

ISBN: 978-1-925234-26-8

Printed in Korea

The Best Food in the Forest

Written by Mi-ae Lee
Illustrated by Yeon-joo Kim
Edited by Joy Cowley

Chef Bear said to the animals in the forest,
"I will make you a most delicious meal."

The animals were very excited.
Chef Bear was an excellent cook.

"What kind of food would you like?"
asked Chef Bear to the animals.

"Salty peanuts!"
said Rabbit.

"Spicy peppers!"
shouted Leopard.

"Sweets!"
said Fox.

Chef Bear put up signs with pictures of peanuts, peppers and sweets. "Line up in front of your favourite sign," said Chef Bear to the animals.

But they all made zigzag lines because they couldn't choose. Elephant stood between two signs. "I like peanuts and peppers," she said.

Chef Bear made them line up in single lines.
"I need to see which line is the longest!"

The animals shifted and stood in order.
The longest line was in front of the sweets sign.
Sweets were the most popular.

"I'll cook something sweet," said Chef Bear.

"Now what shall I cook?" asked Chef Bear. "Can you suggest some ingredients?"

"Fresh meat, please!" shouted Leopard.

"Green vegetables, please!"said Squirrel and Rabbit.

"Fresh fish!"
cried Fox brother
and Fox sister.

Chef Bear told the animals
to bring their favourite ingredients.
As the animals rushed to obey,
Chef Bear called for order.
"Don't pile them up in a heap.
I can't see what is here."

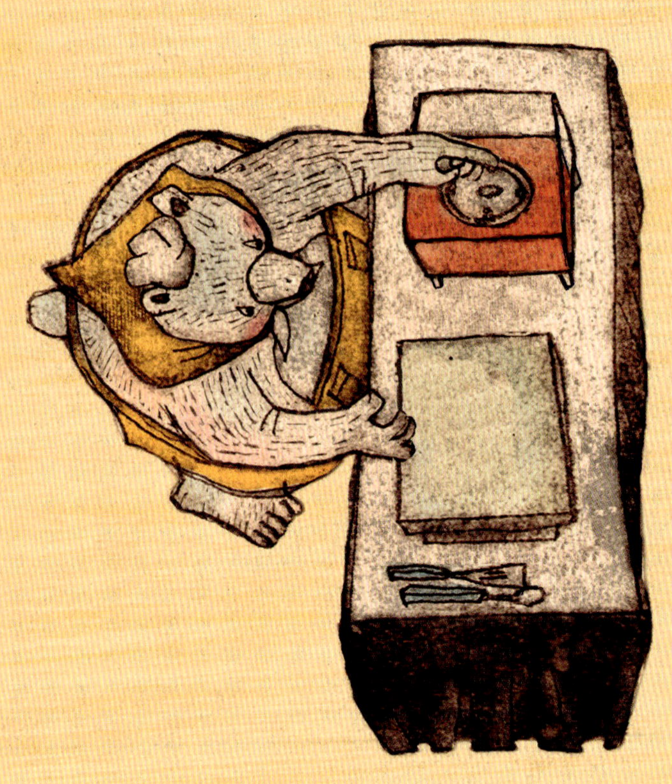

The chef brought some rolls of aluminum foil
and rolled them out on the ground.
"Put meat, vegetables and fish
neatly on the three foil mats."

The meat line and the vegetable line
were the same length.
The fish line was shorter.
"I'll cook meat and vegetables," said Chef Bear.

He said, “You have chosen
the flavour and the ingredients.
How should I cook these?
Use a pan to stir fry the food?
Use a pot to boil the food?
Use a grill to barbecue the food?”

Then Chef Bear got three kinds
of refrigerator magnets with pictures,

one with a pan,

one with a pot,

and one with a grill.

The animals each chose a magnet
and put it on the refrigerator.
There were so many magnets
placed here and there,
that it was difficult to see
which was the most popular.

"Let's arrange them in order,"
said Chef Bear, and he put the magnets
in lines according to their kind.
"The line of the pan magnets is longest.
More of you chose the pan magnet.
So I'll cook your meal in a pan."

Oil

Happily, Chef Bear began to cook.
"I'll choose the name of this meal, myself.
I'll call it the Best Food in the Forest."

Soon the meat and vegetables
were sizzling in the pan.
Chef Bear took a bottle from his pocket.
It was his "Amazing Sweet Sauce".
He put some in the pan.

The animals had a great feast.
“This tastes amazing!” they said.
“It really is the best food in the forest.”

Chef Bear smiled. “It is the best because you all chose it,” he said.